XTREME SPEED

THE WORLD'S FASTEST
TRAINS

A&D Xtreme
BOLD HI-LO NONFICTION

An imprint of Abdo Publishing
abdobooks.com

S.L. HAMILTON

TAKE IT TO
THE XTREME!

GET READY FOR AN XTREME ADVENTURE!
THE PAGES OF THIS BOOK WILL TAKE YOU INTO THE THRILLING
WORLD OF THE FASTEST TRAINS ON EARTH.
WHEN YOU HAVE FINISHED READING THIS BOOK, TAKE THE
XTREME CHALLENGE ON PAGE 45 ABOUT WHAT YOU'VE LEARNED!

ABDOBOOKS.COM

Published by Abdo Publishing, a division of ABDO, PO Box 398166, Minneapolis, Minnesota 55439. Copyright © 2021 by Abdo Consulting Group, Inc. International copyrights reserved in all countries. No part of this book may be reproduced in any form without written permission from the publisher. A&D Xtreme™ is a trademark and logo of Abdo Publishing.

Printed in the United States of America, North Mankato, MN.

032020

092020

Editor: John Hamilton; Copy Editor: Bridget O'Brien

Graphic Design: Sue Hamilton; Imprint Template Design: Dorothy Toth

Cover Design: Victoria Bates

Cover Photo: Alamy

Interior Photos & Illustrations: Alamy-pgs 12-13 & 18-19; Alstom/AGV Italo-pgs 32-33; East Japan Railway Company-pgs 36-37; Eurostar-pgs 30-31; Getty-pgs 10, 20-21, 38-39 & 40-41; Hennie Heymans-pg 25 (inset); History in Full Color-pg 7; Pennsylvania Railroad-pgs 26-27; Queensland Rail-pgs 22-23; Roger Puta-pgs 16-17; Shutterstock-pgs 1, 4-5, 6, 8-9 & 28-29; Siemens-pg 11; Skytrain-pgs 14-15; South African Railway-pgs 24-25; T-Flight-pg 44; Trenitalia-pgs 34-35; US Air Force-pgs 42-43.

LIBRARY OF CONGRESS CONTROL NUMBER: 2019956098

PUBLISHER'S CATALOGING-IN-PUBLICATION DATA

Names: Hamilton, S.L., author.

Title: The world's fastest trains / by S.L. Hamilton

Description: Minneapolis, Minnesota : Abdo Publishing, 2021 | Series: Xtreme speed | Includes online resources and index

Identifiers: ISBN 9781532193958 (lib. bdg.) | ISBN 9781098212735 (ebook)

Subjects: LCSH: Speed--Juvenile literature. | Railroads--Speed records--Juvenile literature. | Motor vehicles--Juvenile literature. | Transportation--Juvenile literature.

Classification: DDC 629.046--dc23

TABLE OF CONTENTS

CHAPTER 1

THE WORLD'S FASTEST
TRAINS

Some trains are traditional wheeled vehicles. Others rise above the tracks, using powerful magnets to produce incredible speed.

The fastest trains run at speeds of 375 mph (604 kph) or more. These blurs of speed carry people and products from place to place, sometimes as fast as airplanes.

A bullet train races into a station.

CHAPTER 2

HISTORY

Trains were first created to carry products. Ancient Greeks and Egyptians used horses or bulls to pull simple train cars. Steam engines first powered trains in England in the early 1800s.

George Stephenson's 1829 steam-powered Rocket had a top speed of 28 mph (45 kph).

Soon, train tracks were laid all across Europe. In the United States, tracks connected the eastern and western coasts in 1869. Before long, train travel was common for passengers and goods. The faster the train, the more popular and successful it became.

On May 10, 1869, Union Pacific and Central Pacific Railroad workers celebrated the first transcontinental railroad at Promontory Summit, Utah.

CHAPTER 3
ENGINEERS

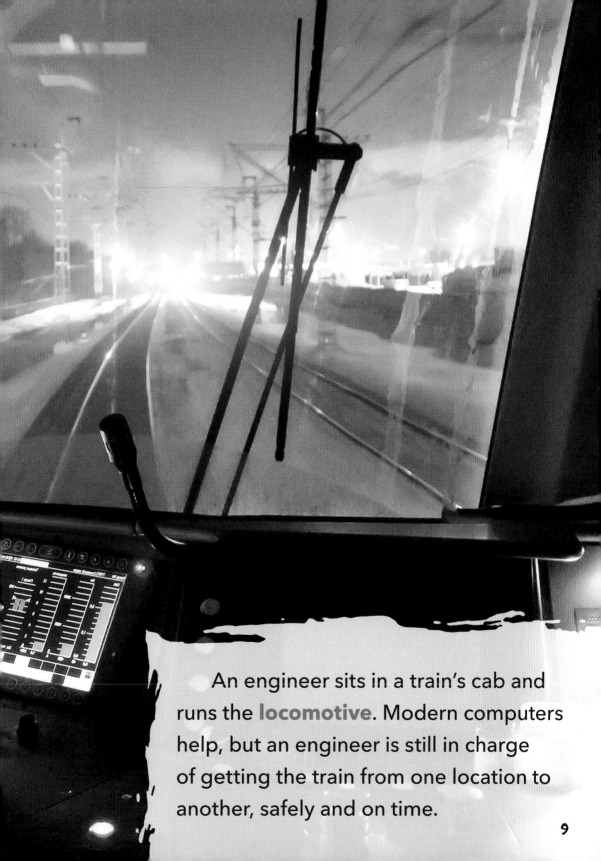

An engineer sits in a train's cab and runs the **locomotive**. Modern computers help, but an engineer is still in charge of getting the train from one location to another, safely and on time.

CHAPTER 4

TRAIN TUNNELS

Many trains travel at high speed through underground tunnels. Tunnel boring machines (TBMs), or "moles," dig through everything from hard rock to sand to make these huge tunnels.

A TBM breaks into a second shaft at the Gotthard Base Tunnel in 2010.

When the Gotthard Base Tunnel opened in 2016, it was the longest and deepest train tunnel ever built.

Switzerland's Gotthard Base Tunnel runs for 35.5 miles (57 km) and as deep as 1.5 miles (2.4 km) through the Swiss Alps. High-speed passenger and freight trains race through the tunnel at speeds up to 155 mph (250 kph).

CHAPTER 5

SPEED BEASTS

A funicular train travels up very steep tracks. Switzerland's Stoosbahn Funicular climbs 2,441 feet (744 m) to the mountain resort of Stoos. The train reaches speeds of 22 mph (36 kph). It takes only 4 minutes for it to climb the steepest train track in the world.

TOP SPEED RANGE
22-79 mph
(36-127 kph)

SPEED BEAST TYPES
Funicular, Monorail,
Freight Train

XTREME FACT

The Stoos funicular's round
carriages rotate to keep the
floor flat for passengers as
the train climbs.

XTREME FACT

China's Skytrain is also called a suspension train.

A monorail train runs on a single elevated track. China's monorail Skytrain reaches speeds of 40 mph (64 kph). It zips up to 500 passengers through Hancheng City. The track is 16 feet (5 m) above the ground.

The world's fastest freight train was the Atchison, Topeka and Santa Fe Railway's Super C. It had a top speed of 79 mph (127 kph).

The Super C ran from Chicago, Illinois, to Los Angeles, California. It carried from 1-20 cars full of freight. The Super C made its last trip in May 1976, but its record stands.

One of the Super C's main customers was the US Post Office.

CHAPTER 6

SPEED MONSTERS

North America's fastest passenger train is Amtrak's Acela Express. It reaches 125 mph (201 kph).

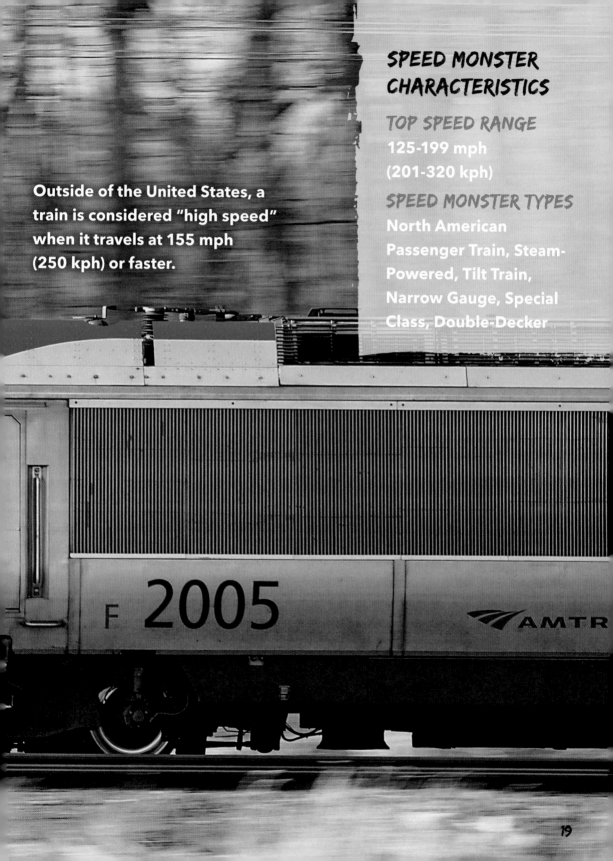

SPEED MONSTER CHARACTERISTICS

TOP SPEED RANGE
**125-199 mph
(201-320 kph)**

SPEED MONSTER TYPES
**North American
Passenger Train, Steam-
Powered, Tilt Train,
Narrow Gauge, Special
Class, Double-Decker**

Outside of the United States, a train is considered "high speed" when it travels at 155 mph (250 kph) or faster.

F 2005

AMTR

The fastest steam-powered **locomotive** was London and North Eastern Railway's Mallard. It raced down a track near Grantham, England, at 126 mph (203 kph) on July 3, 1938.

Mallard covered nearly 1.5 million miles (2.4 million km) before being retired in 1963. Today, the train is on display at the National Railway Museum in York, England.

A **tilt train** is able to take curves at greater speeds. The fastest electric tilt train speed was set in Australia. Queensland Rail's Tilt Train reached 130 mph (210 kph) in May 1999.

Tilt Train

QR

5402

Engine E1525's speed record occurred on a track made for the train between Westonaria and Midway, South Africa.

XTREME FACT

Engine E1525 had a special nose cone designed for the high-speed tests.

South African Railways built an experimental Class 6E1 electric engine designed for high speeds. On October 31, 1978, Engine E1525 made the **narrow gauge** world rail speed record by reaching 152 mph (245 kph).

Pennsylvania Railroad (PRR) built a special class steam **locomotive** in 1939. The S1 6100 had a unique wheel arrangement that allowed the long, heavy locomotive to reach a top speed of 156 mph (251 kph).

After the S1 reached its record speed, PRR got a speeding ticket for going faster than the tracks allowed.

The S1 locomotive was nicknamed "The Big Engine."

27

Euroduplex trains run across France, Switzerland, Germany, and Luxembourg.

Euroduplex trains are the fastest trains that carry more than 1,000 people. These big **double-decker** trains reach a top speed of 199 mph (320 kph).

CHAPTER 7

SPEED DEMONS

Europe's high-speed Eurostar e320 carries up to 750 passengers to and from England, France, and Belgium. It travels through the "Chunnel," an underwater tunnel built below the English Channel. The train is named for its normal speed of 320 kph (199 mph). In 2003, Eurostar train 3313/14 reached a record speed of 208 mph (335 kph).

SPEED DEMON CHARACTERISTICS

TOP SPEED RANGE
208-250 mph
(335-400 kph)

SPEED DEMON TYPES
750 Passenger,
250+ Passenger, 500
Passenger, Bullet Train

Europe's fastest passenger train carrying about 250 people is AGV Italo. It travels between Rome and Naples, Italy, reaching a top speed of 224 mph (360 kph).

XTREME FACT

Frecciarossa 1000 is also known as "Red Arrow."

Italy's Frecciarossa 1000 carries up to 500 people on high-speed travels. On February 26, 2016, it reached a record speed of 245 mph (394 kph) while traveling from Torino to Milan.

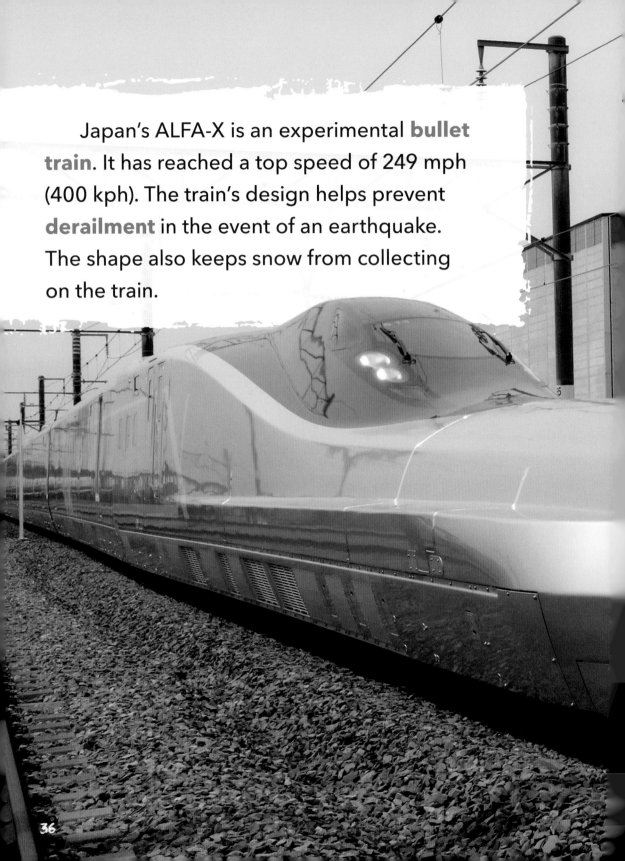

Japan's ALFA-X is an experimental **bullet train**. It has reached a top speed of 249 mph (400 kph). The train's design helps prevent **derailment** in the event of an earthquake. The shape also keeps snow from collecting on the train.

**ALFA-X stands for Advanced Labs for
Frontline Activity in rail eXperimentation.**

CHAPTER 8

SPEED FREAKS

China's Qingdao **maglev** uses a magnetic field to make it one of the fastest trains in the world. This magnetic levitation train has no wheels and no contact with the track. It moves at a top speed of 373 mph (600 kph).

SPEED FREAK CHARACTERISTICS

TOP SPEED RANGE

**373-6,453 mph
(600-10,385 kph)**

SPEED FREAK TYPES

**Maglev, L0 Series,
Rocket Sled**

A maglev train takes only about four minutes to go from zero to its top speed.

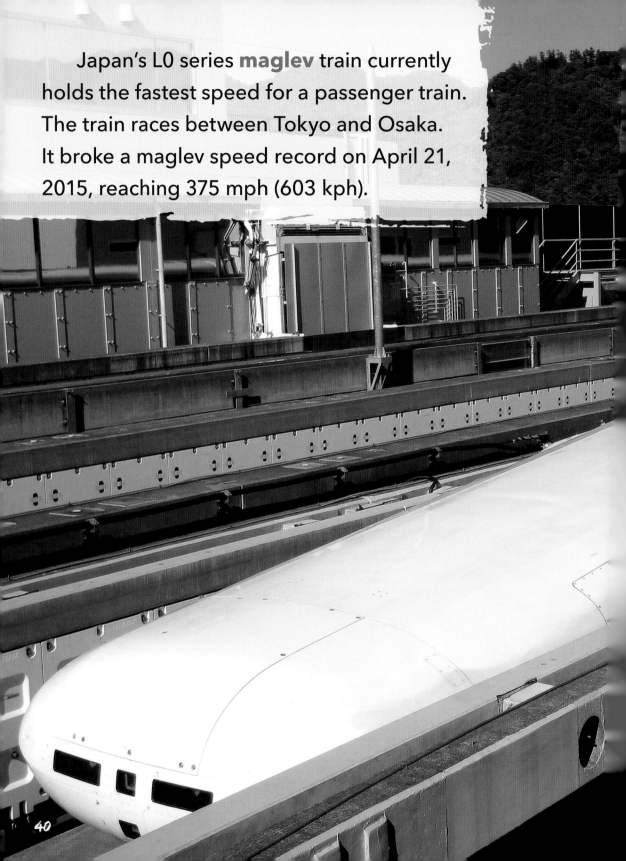

Japan's L0 series **maglev** train currently holds the fastest speed for a passenger train. The train races between Tokyo and Osaka. It broke a maglev speed record on April 21, 2015, reaching 375 mph (603 kph).

XTREME FACT

A L0 series train has a 49-foot (15-m) -long nose. It helps move the train more easily through the air and increases speed.

A **rocket sled** reached 6,453 mph (10,385 kph) at Holloman Air Force Base in New Mexico on April 29, 2003. The experimental train used sliding pads that curved around a railed track to keep it from **derailing** at high speeds.

CHAPTER 9

FUTURE CONCEPTS

American Elon Musk is working on a **transonic** train called Hyperloop. It may reach 760 mph (1,200 kph). China is working on T-Flight. This **hypersonic** "flying train" could have a top speed of 2,485 mph (4,000 kph). It would be five times faster than today's commercial jets!

XTREME CHALLENGE

TAKE THE QUIZ BELOW AND
PUT WHAT YOU'VE LEARNED TO THE TEST!

1) What does a train engineer do?

2) What is a TBM? What is its nickname?

3) What is a funicular train?

4) What are the most number of passengers on one of today's trains?

5) Why does a tilt train tilt?

6) What does "maglev" stand for?

7) Has a train ever gone faster than the speed of sound (770 mph/1,238 kph)?

8) What country is working on a hypersonic train? How fast could it go?

GLOSSARY

bullet train – Another name for a high-speed train. Its shape and speed are like a bullet.

derailment – When a train's wheels run off the rail. This often results in a serious accident with train cars on their sides on the ground next to the track.

double-decker – Two levels. A double-decker train or bus has seating for passengers on a top and bottom level.

hypersonic – Extremely high speed between 3,821-7,643 mph (6,150-12,300 kph).

locomotive – A rail transport vehicle that provides the power for a train. Locomotives usually pull train cars from the front, but they may also be at the back, or have one at the front and one at the back.

maglev – Magnetic levitation. A type of train that uses magnetic fields to move itself forward. The train floats just above a track. This type of train is very fast.

narrow gauge – A track that is narrower than a standard track. Most narrow-gauge railways are 24-42 inches (600-1,067 mm) wide, while a standard track is about 56.5 inches (1,435 mm).

rocket sled – A wheelless sled that uses sliding pads or "slippers" to hold it on a railed track. A rocket sled currently holds the land-based speed record for a railed vehicle.

tilt train – A train that tilts to the inside of a curve to keep passengers and people from being thrown off balance. This allows the train to take curves at a faster speed.

transonic – Speed that moves "through" the speed of sound. Transonic speed is about 600-768 mph (965-1,236 kph).

ONLINE RESOURCES

Booklinks
NONFICTION NETWORK
FREE! ONLINE NONFICTION RESOURCES

To learn more about the world's fastest trains, please visit **abdobooklinks.com** or scan this QR code. These links are routinely monitored and updated to provide the most current information available.

INDEX